LAND OF LIBERTY

AMERICA'S PEOPLE

LYNN M. STONE

Rourke
Publishing LLC
Vero Beach, Florida 32964

www.rourkepublishing.com

PHOTO CREDITS: All pictures by the author except page16 © Breck Kent; pages 9, 10 © Jerry Hennen; page 15 © Joseph Sohm/PhotoSpin

Cover Photo: *Americans united, middle schoolers in Wheaton, Illinois, take a classroom timeout to form the American flag.*

Editor: Frank Sloan

Cover and page design by Nicola Stratford

Library of Congress Cataloging-in-Publication Data

Stone, Lynn M.
  America's people / Lynn M. Stone.
     p. cm. — (Land of liberty)
Summary: Discusses how the various ethnic groups that settled in the United States throughout its history contributed to the evolution of a distinctly American character. Includes bibliographical references and index.
  ISBN 1-58952-309-1 (hardcover)
 1. Ethnology—United States—Juvenile literature. 2. United States—Population--Juvenile literature. 3. United States—Social conditions—Juvenile literature. 4. United States—Social life and customs—Juvenile literature. [1. Ethnology—United States. 2. United States—Population. 3. United States—Social life and customs.] I. Title.

  E184.A1 S87 2002
  305.8'00973—dc21

                                                         2002004153

Printed in the USA

MP/W

Table of Contents

People with ancestors from all over the world have united to become Americans.

People of America

Perhaps you have heard America called a "melting pot." That's because Americans have come from many different countries and groups of people. Much of America's character comes from the many different people who live there. In fact, in many ways, America's people are a mirror of the world around her.

The 2000 Census

America's 2000 **census** showed a **population** of 281,421,966. That's almost three hundred million people. Among the world's nations, only China and India have more people.

About 75 of 100 Americans live in cities like Chicago and its suburbs.

The People Who Make Up America

Nearly 71 of every 100 have a European background. About 12 and one-half of each 100 are **Hispanic**. Hispanics come from Mexico and the nations of Central and South America.

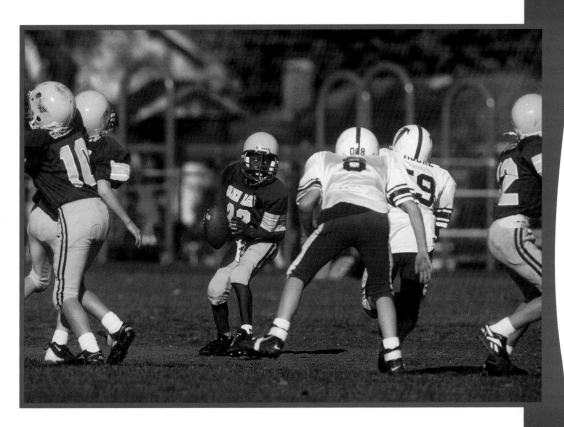

Americans from all walks of life have learned how to live and play together.

Just less than 12 and one-half of each 100 are of African **descent.** About 3 and one-half of every 100 Americans are of Asian background. Asian Americans are largely from China, Japan, India, Korea, Vietnam, Pakistan, and the Philippines.

Native American peoples accounted for less than 1 person per 100 in 2000.

A Mexican American dances at a traditional summer festival.

Some Native Americans keep many of their customs, like this tribal dance.

The First Natives

The first people in America were the **native** peoples. The Native Americans of northern Alaska call themselves **Inuit.** The other native peoples are the many tribes of American Indians.

Europeans may have "discovered" America long before Christopher Columbus's voyage of 1492. But it was only after that voyage that Europeans began to settle in America.

Settlers in America

The first settlers from Europe were small numbers of people from Spain. A few French and many English settlers followed.

By the mid-1600s, England had several colonies in America. Smaller groups of settlers arrived from many European countries over the next 350 years.

Visitors tour the stone fort built by early Spanish settlers in St. Augustine, Florida.

Most African Americans are descendants of people who were brought to America as slaves from Africa.

In the 1600s some of the new English colonies began importing Africans to be slaves. These people were the **ancestors** of most African Americans.

Speaking the Same Language

Chinese and other Asian groups began arriving in the United States in the mid-1800s.

Most people who arrived from other lands soon learned to speak English. Having the same language helped many different people unite in their new land.

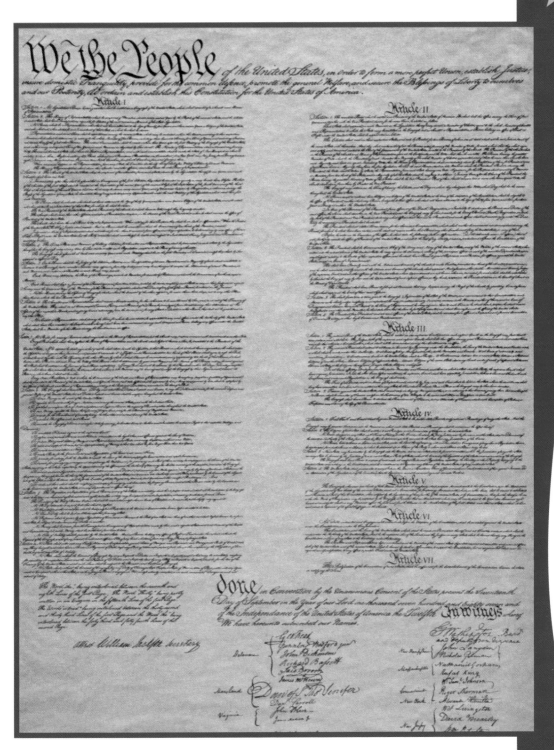

The language and ideals of America's early English settlers helped shape the new nation.

War memorials, like the Vietnam Veterans' Memorial, remind Americans that liberty can cost lives.

Life in America

Americans live in a land of liberty. Americans are guaranteed many basic rights within the law. American laws allow many freedoms. Americans are free to worship, travel, speak, and express themselves as they please.

Americans at Work

Americans are some of the best educated people in the world. About 75 of every 100 American students finish high school. That prepares Americans for a variety of jobs in factories, offices, schools, farms, and other places.

These people became marine biologists through American education.

American workers and natural resources help the nation lead the world in goods and services produced.

American workers produce more goods and services than any other nation. A third of the world's food exports come from America.

Americans at Play

Americans spend their free time doing many different things. They love boating and sunbathing, reading, and driving. They enjoy movies, music, and sports. They go to stage plays, zoos, aquariums, concerts, and art museums.

Americans love sports, including this one of their own making—baseball!

Entertainment such as jazz and musical comedy began in the United States. And where would Americans at play be without three more favorite inventions: baseball, football, and basketball?

Americans enjoy outdoor recreation.

Glossary

ancestor (ANN sess tuhr) – a person of your family line who lived long before you

census (SENN suss) – an official counting of people

descent (dee SENT) – one's racial background, such as being of African descent

Hispanic (his SPAN ick) – referring to people of Spanish background

Inuit (INN you it) – Native Americans of northern Alaska

native (NAY tuv) – one whose people group, such as American Indians, was in a place before settlers from countries arrived there

population (POP you LAY shun) – the total number of people in a place

Index

Further Reading

Lawlor, Veronica. *I Was Dreaming to Come to America.* Penguin USA, 1997

Long, Cathryn. *Crosswords America: American History to 1900.* GA Publishing, 1998

Maestro, Betsy. *Coming to America: The Story of Immigration.* Scholastic, 1996

Websites to Visit

Smithsonian National Museum of American History at:
    http://americanhistory.si.edu/
Internet African American History Challenge at:
    http://www.brightmoments.com/blackhistory/
PBS: The New Americans at http://www.pbs.org/kcet/newamericans/

About the Author

Lynn Stone is the author of over 400 children's nonfiction books. He is a talented natural history photographer as well. Lynn, a former teacher, travels worldwide to photograph wildlife in its natural habitat.